This book belongs to
_____

This book is dedicated to my children - Mikey, Kobe, and Jojo.

Copyright © 2025 Grow Grit Press LLC. All rights reserved. No part of this book may be reproduced in any form without permission in writing from the publisher. Please send bulk order requests to info@ninjalifehacks.tv

Paperback ISBN: 979-8-89614-048-1
Hardcover ISBN: 979-8-89614-050-4
eBook ISBN: 979-8-89614-049-8

Printed and bound in the USA.
NinjaLifeHacks.tv

Ninja Life Hacks®
by Mary Nhin

Scared Ninja

A Children's Book About Facing Fears

Ninja Life Hacks®
by Mary Nhin

When it's time to try something new, like climbing a rock wall, I feel scared. I remember to take a deep breath, imagine I'm in a safe place, and tell myself I can do it. Then, I start climbing slowly, and soon I'm at the top!

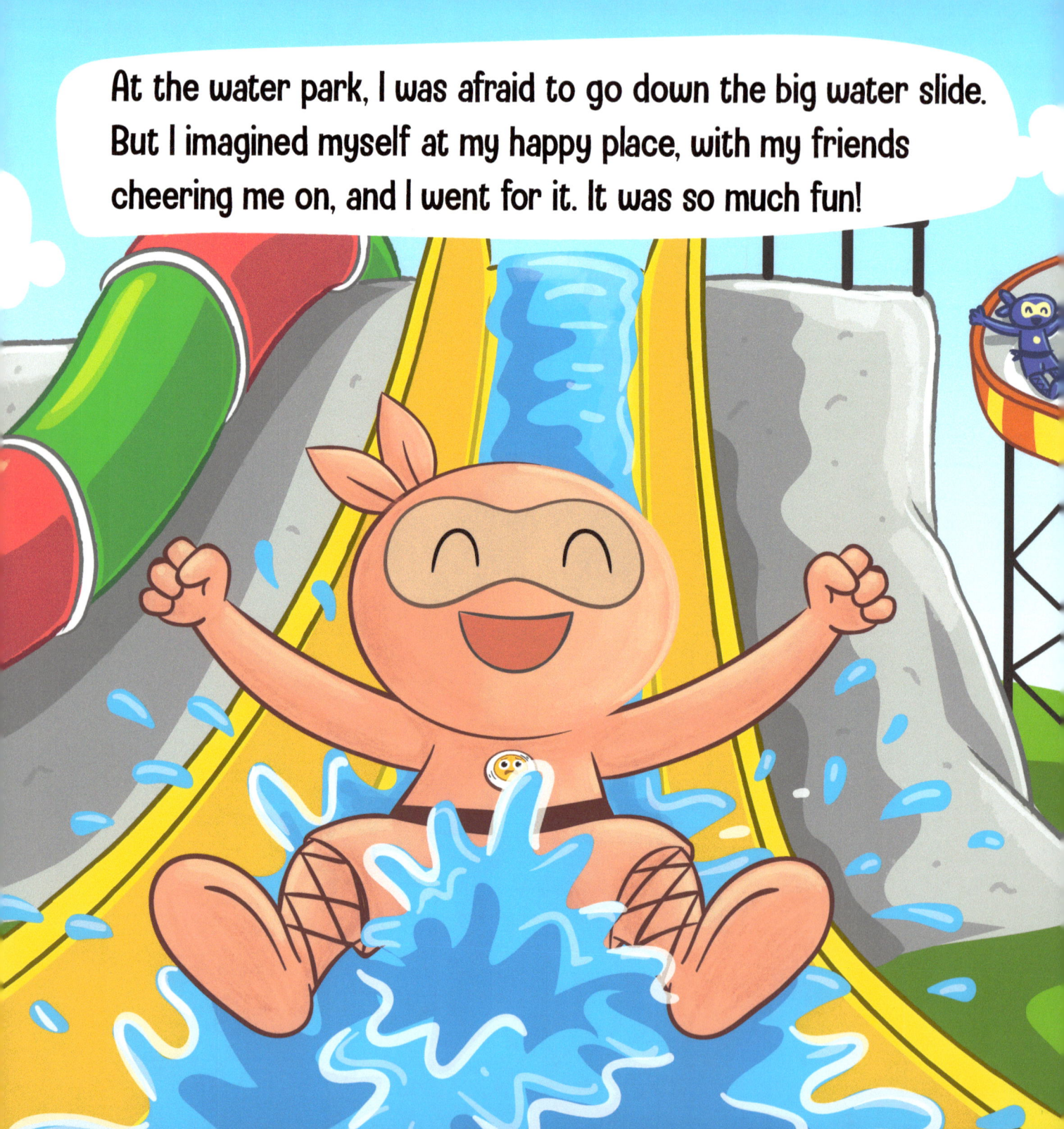

Remembering the **L.I.O.N.** hack could be your secret weapon against fear!

Check out the fun Scared Ninja lesson plans at ninjalifehacks.tv

I love to hear from my readers. Email me your feedback or thoughts on what my next story should be at info@ninjalifehacks.tv   Yours truly, Mary

 @marynhin   @GrowGrit
#NinjaLifeHacks

 Mary Nhin   Ninja Life Hacks

 Ninja Life Hacks

 @officialninjalifehacks

www.ingramcontent.com/pod-product-compliance
Lightning Source LLC
LaVergne TN
LVHW070437070526
838199LV00015B/530